ALTO SAX

The **BIG BOOK** of

alto sax songs

AVAILABLE FOR:
Flute, Clarinet, Alto Sax, Tenor Sax, Trumpet,
Horn, Trombone, Violin, Viola, and Cello

ISBN: 978-1-4234-2665-3

HAL•LEONARD®

Visit Hal Leonard Online at
www.halleonard.com

Contact Us:
Hal Leonard
7777 West Bluemound Road
Milwaukee, WI 53213
Email: info@halleonard.com

In Europe contact:
Hal Leonard Europe Limited
42 Wigmore Street
Marylebone, London, W1U 2RN
Email: info@halleonardeurope.com

In Australia contact:
Hal Leonard Australia Pty. Ltd.
4 Lentara Court
Cheltenham, Victoria, 3192 Australia
Email: info@halleonard.com.au

CONTENTS

ALL MY LOVING

from A HARD DAY'S NIGHT

ALTO SAX

Words and Music by JOHN LENNON
and PAUL McCARTNEY

ALL THE SMALL THINGS

ALTO SAX

Words and Music by TOM DE LONGE
and MARK HOPPUS

ALLEY CAT

ALTO SAX

By FRANK BJORN

ANOTHER ONE BITES THE DUST

ALTO SAX

Words and Music by
JOHN DEACON

AMERICA

from the Motion Picture THE JAZZ SINGER

ALTO SAX

Words and Music by
NEIL DIAMOND

1.
2.

ANY DREAM WILL DO

from JOSEPH AND THE AMAZING TECHNICOLOR® DREAMCOAT

ALTO SAX

Music by ANDREW LLOYD WEBBER
Lyrics by TIM RICE

BE TRUE TO YOUR SCHOOL

ALTO SAX

Words and Music by BRIAN WILSON
and MIKE LOVE

Slowly

BAD DAY

ALTO SAX

Words and Music by
DANIEL POWTER

Moderate groove

D.S. al Coda
CODA

BARELY BREATHING

ALTO SAX

Words and Music by
DUNCAN SHEIK

Moderately

1.
2., 3.
To Coda
3
D.S. al Coda
CODA

(It's A)
BEAUTIFUL MORNING

ALTO SAX

Words and Music by FELIX CAVALIERE
and EDWARD BRIGATI, JR.

BEAUTY AND THE BEAST

from Walt Disney's BEAUTY AND THE BEAST

ALTO SAX

Lyrics by HOWARD ASHMAN
Music by ALAN MENKEN

Moderately slow

BEYOND THE SEA

ALTO SAX

Words and Music by CHARLES TRENET,
ALBERT LASRY and JACK LAWRENCE

BLACKBIRD

ALTO SAX

Words and Music by JOHN LENNON
and PAUL McCARTNEY

BLUE SUEDE SHOES

ALTO SAX

Words and Music by
CARL LEE PERKINS

BOOGIE WOOGIE BUGLE BOY

from BUCK PRIVATES

ALTO SAX

Words and Music by DON RAYE
and HUGHIE PRINCE

THE BRADY BUNCH

Theme from the Paramount Television Series THE BRADY BUNCH

ALTO SAX

Words and Music by SHERWOOD SCHWARTZ
and FRANK DEVOL

Happily

BUTTERFLY KISSES

ALTO SAX

Words and Music by BOB CARLISLE
and RANDY THOMAS

BREAKING FREE

from the Disney Channel Original Movie HIGH SCHOOL MUSICAL

ALTO SAX

Words and Music by
JAMIE HOUSTON

CABARET

from the Musical CABARET

ALTO SAX

Words by FRED EBB
Music by JOHN KANDER

CALIFORNIA DREAMIN'

ALTO SAX

Words and Music by JOHN PHILLIPS
and MICHELLE PHILLIPS

CANDLE IN THE WIND

ALTO SAX

Words and Music by ELTON JOHN
and BERNIE TAUPIN

CHIM CHIM CHER-EE

from Walt Disney's MARY POPPINS

ALTO SAX

Words and Music by RICHARD M. SHERMAN
and ROBERT B. SHERMAN

Lightly, with gusto

CLOCKS

ALTO SAX

Words and Music by GUY BERRYMAN, JON BUCKLAND, WILL CHAMPION and CHRIS MARTIN

(They Long to Be)

CLOSE TO YOU

ALTO SAX

Lyric by HAL DAVID
Music by BURT BACHARACH

Slowly, with a steady beat

COLORS OF THE WIND

from Walt Disney's POCAHONTAS

ALTO SAX

Music by ALAN MENKEN
Lyrics by STEPHEN SCHWARTZ

COME FLY WITH ME

ALTO SAX

Words by SAMMY CAHN
Music by JAMES VAN HEUSEN

COPACABANA
(At the Copa)
from Barry Manilow's COPACABANA

ALTO SAX

Music by BARRY MANILOW
Lyric by BRUCE SUSSMAN and JACK FELDMAN

Moderately, with a Latin feel

DO-RE-MI

from THE SOUND OF MUSIC

ALTO SAX

Lyrics by OSCAR HAMMERSTEIN II
Music by RICHARD RODGERS

DO WAH DIDDY DIDDY

ALTO SAX

Words and Music by JEFF BARRY
and ELLIE GREENWICH

(Sittin' On)

THE DOCK OF THE BAY

ALTO SAX

Words and Music by STEVE CROPPER
and OTIS REDDING

DON'T BE CRUEL
(To a Heart That's True)

ALTO SAX

Words and Music by OTIS BLACKWELL
and ELVIS PRESLEY

DON'T LET THE SUN GO DOWN ON ME

ALTO SAX

Words and Music by ELTON JOHN
and BERNIE TAUPIN

Slow Rock

DON'T SPEAK

ALTO SAX

Words and Music by ERIC STEFANI
and GWEN STEFANI

Moderately

D.S. al Coda
CODA
3
small notes optional

DRIFT AWAY

ALTO SAX

Words and Music by
MENTOR WILLIAMS

Moderately fast

DUKE OF EARL

ALTO SAX

Words and Music by EARL EDWARDS,
EUGENE DIXON and BERNICE WILLIAMS

Moderately

THEME FROM E.T. (THE EXTRA-TERRESTRIAL)

from the Universal Picture E.T. (THE EXTRA-TERRESTRIAL)

ALTO SAX

Music by
JOHN WILLIAMS

EDELWEISS

from THE SOUND OF MUSIC

ALTO SAX

Lyrics by OSCAR HAMMERSTEIN II
Music by RICHARD RODGERS

Gently

EVERY BREATH YOU TAKE

ALTO SAX

Music and Lyrics by
STING

EVERYTHING IS BEAUTIFUL

ALTO SAX

Words and Music by
RAY STEVENS

Moderately fast

FALLIN'

ALTO SAX

Words and Music by
ALICIA KEYS

1., 2.
3.

FIELDS OF GOLD

ALTO SAX

Music and Lyrics by
STING

FLY LIKE AN EAGLE

ALTO SAX

Words and Music by
STEVE MILLER

Moderately, in 2

FOR ONCE IN MY LIFE

ALTO SAX

Words by RONALD MILLER
Music by ORLANDO MURDEN

FOREVER YOUNG

ALTO SAX

Words and Music by ROD STEWART,
JIM CREGAN, KEVIN SAVIGAR and BOB DYLAN

Driving beat

FUN, FUN, FUN

ALTO SAX

Words and Music by BRIAN WILSON
and MIKE LOVE

Bright Rock

THE GIRL FROM IPANEMA

(Garôta de Ipanema)

ALTO SAX

Music by ANTONIO CARLOS JOBIM
English Words by NORMAN GIMBEL
Original Words by VINICIUS DE MORAES

GOD BLESS THE U.S.A

ALTO SAX

Words and Music by
LEE GREENWOOD

GONNA BUILD A MOUNTAIN

from the Musical Production STOP THE WORLD – I WANT TO GET OFF

ALTO SAX

Words and Music by LESLIE BRICUSSE
and ANTHONY NEWLEY

Moderately bright

GOODBYE YELLOW BRICK ROAD

ALTO SAX

Words and Music by ELTON JOHN
and BERNIE TAUPIN

Moderately slow, in 2

GREEN GREEN GRASS OF HOME

ALTO SAX

Words and Music by
CURLY PUTMAN

HAPPY DAYS

Theme from the Paramount Television Series HAPPY DAYS

ALTO SAX

Words by NORMAN GIMBEL
Music by CHARLES FOX

Brightly

HAVE I TOLD YOU LATELY

ALTO SAX

Words and Music by
VAN MORRISON

HEART AND SOUL

from the Paramount Short Subject A SONG IS BORN

ALTO SAX

Words by FRANK LOESSER
Music by HOAGY CARMICHAEL

HOGAN'S HEROES MARCH
from the Television Series HOGAN'S HEROES

ALTO SAX

By JERRY FIELDING

Moderately

HERE WITHOUT YOU

ALTO SAX

Words and Music by MATT ROBERTS,
BRAD ARNOLD, CHRISTOPHER HENDERSON
and ROBERT HARRELL

Moderate Rock

1.
2.
4

I DREAMED A DREAM

from LES MISÉRABLES

ALTO SAX

Music by CLAUDE-MICHEL SCHÖNBERG
Lyrics by ALAIN BOUBLIL, JEAN-MARC NATEL
and HERBERT KRETZMER

I HEARD IT THROUGH THE GRAPEVINE

ALTO SAX

Words and Music by NORMAN J. WHITFIELD
and BARRETT STRONG

I SAY A LITTLE PRAYER

ALTO SAX

Lyric by HAL DAVID
Music by BURT BACHARACH

Moderately fast

I WHISTLE A HAPPY TUNE

from THE KING AND I

ALTO SAX

Lyrics by OSCAR HAMMERSTEIN II
Music by RICHARD RODGERS

Brightly

I WILL REMEMBER YOU

Theme from THE BROTHERS McMULLEN

ALTO SAX

Words and Music by SARAH McLACHLAN, SEAMUS EGAN and DAVE MERENDA

Moderately slow

I WRITE THE SONGS

ALTO SAX

Words and Music by
BRUCE JOHNSTON

Slow Ballad

I'M POPEYE THE SAILOR MAN

Theme from the Paramount Cartoon POPEYE THE SAILOR

ALTO SAX

Words and Music by
SAMMY LERNER

IF I EVER LOSE MY FAITH IN YOU

ALTO SAX

Music and Lyrics by
STING

IMAGINE

ALTO SAX

Words and Music by
JOHN LENNON

IT'S MY LIFE

ALTO SAX

Words and Music by JON BON JOVI,
RICHARD SAMBORA and MARTIN SANDBERG

Moderately

IT'S STILL ROCK AND ROLL TO ME

ALTO SAX

Words and Music by
BILLY JOEL

JAILHOUSE ROCK

ALTO SAX

Words and Music by JERRY LEIBER
and MIKE STOLLER

Moderately

JOY TO THE WORLD

ALTO SAX

Words and Music by
HOYT AXTON

Moderate Gospel Rock

JUMP, JIVE AN' WAIL

ALTO SAX

Words and Music by
LOUIS PRIMA

KANSAS CITY

ALTO SAX

Words and Music by JERRY LEIBER and MIKE STOLLER

Blues tempo (♫ = ♩♪ triplet)

KOKOMO

from the Motion Picture COCKTAIL

ALTO SAX

Words and Music by MIKE LOVE, TERRY MELCHER, JOHN PHILLIPS and SCOTT McKENZIE

Moderately bright

LET 'EM IN

ALTO SAX

Words and Music by
PAUL and LINDA McCARTNEY

Moderately

LET'S STAY TOGETHER

ALTO SAX

Words and Music by AL GREEN,
WILLIE MITCHELL and AL JACKSON, JR.

LIKE A ROCK

ALTO SAX

Words and Music by
BOB SEGER

D.S. al Coda
3
3
CODA
3

LIVIN' LA VIDA LOCA

ALTO SAX

Words and Music by ROBI ROSA
and DESMOND CHILD

Fast, with a steady beat

LOVE AND MARRIAGE

ALTO SAX

Words by SAMMY CAHN
Music by JAMES VAN HEUSEN

LOVE STORY

Theme from the Paramount Picture LOVE STORY

ALTO SAX

Music by FRANCIS LAI

MAGGIE MAY

ALTO SAX

Words and Music by ROD STEWART
and MARTIN QUITTENTON

Moderately bright

MAKING OUR DREAMS COME TRUE

Theme from the Paramount Television Series LAVERNE AND SHIRLEY

ALTO SAX

Words by NORMAN GIMBEL
Music by CHARLES FOX

MAYBE I'M AMAZED

ALTO SAX

Words and Music by
PAUL McCARTNEY

Moderately

MICHELLE

ALTO SAX

Words and Music by JOHN LENNON
and PAUL McCARTNEY

MICKEY MOUSE MARCH

from Walt Disney's THE MICKEY MOUSE CLUB

ALTO SAX

Words and Music by
JIMMIE DODD

MISSION: IMPOSSIBLE THEME

From the Paramount Television Series MISSION: IMPOSSIBLE

ALTO SAX

By LALO SCHIFRIN

Moderately, with drive

MISTER SANDMAN

ALTO SAX

Lyric and Music by
PAT BALLARD

MOON RIVER

from the Paramount Picture BREAKFAST AT TIFFANY'S

ALTO SAX

Words by JOHNNY MERCER
Music by HENRY MANCINI

MY HEART WILL GO ON

(Love Theme from 'Titanic')

from the Paramount and Twentieth Century Fox Motion Picture TITANIC

ALTO SAX

Music by JAMES HORNER
Lyric by WILL JENNINGS

Moderately

MY WAY

ALTO SAX

English Words by PAUL ANKA
Original French Words by GILLES THIBAULT
Music by JACQUES REVAUX and CLAUDE FRANCOIS

NA NA HEY HEY KISS HIM GOODBYE

ALTO SAX

Words and Music by ARTHUR FRASHUER DALE,
PAUL ROGER LEKA and GARY CARLA

ON BROADWAY

ALTO SAX

Words and Music by BARRY MANN,
CYNTHIA WEIL, MIKE STOLLER and JERRY LEIBER

Moderately

PEPPERMINT TWIST

ALTO SAX

Words and Music by JOSEPH DiNICOLA
and HENRY GLOVER

POCKETFUL OF MIRACLES

ALTO SAX

Words by SAMMY CAHN
Music by JAMES VAN HEUSEN

Moderately, with a lilt

PUFF THE MAGIC DRAGON

ALTO SAX

Words and Music by LENNY LIPTON
and PETER YARROW

Moderately

PUT YOUR HAND IN THE HAND

ALTO SAX

Words and Music by
GENE MacLELLAN

QUIET NIGHTS OF QUIET STARS

(Corcovado)

ALTO SAX

English Words by GENE LEES
Original Words and Music by ANTONIO CARLOS JOBIM

Moderately slow

ROCK AROUND THE CLOCK

ALTO SAX

Words and Music by MAX C. FREEDMAN
and JIMMY DeKNIGHT

Moderately

ROCK WITH YOU

ALTO SAX

Words and Music by
ROD TEMPERTON

Moderate Rock

SATIN DOLL

ALTO SAX

By DUKE ELLINGTON

Medium Swing

SAVE THE BEST FOR LAST

ALTO SAX

Words and Music by PHIL GALDSTON,
JON LIND and WENDY WALDMAN

THEME FROM "SCHINDLER'S LIST"

from the Universal Motion Picture SCHINDLER'S LIST

ALTO SAX

Music by JOHN WILLIAMS

SHE WILL BE LOVED

ALTO SAX

Words and Music by ADAM LEVINE
and JAMES VALENTINE

SING

from SESAME STREET

ALTO SAX

Words and Music by
JOE RAPOSO

Moderately

SO LONG, FAREWELL

from THE SOUND OF MUSIC

ALTO SAX

Lyrics by OSCAR HAMMERSTEIN II
Music by RICHARD RODGERS

SOMEWHERE OUT THERE

from AN AMERICAN TAIL

ALTO SAX

Music by BARRY MANN and JAMES HORNER
Lyric by CYNTHIA WEIL

SPANISH FLEA

ALTO SAX

Words and Music by
JULIUS WECHTER

STACY'S MOM

ALTO SAX

Words and Music by CHRIS COLLINGWOOD
and ADAM SCHLESINGER

SUNRISE, SUNSET

from the Musical FIDDLER ON THE ROOF

ALTO SAX

Words by SHELDON HARNICK
Music by JERRY BOCK

Moderately slow Waltz tempo

TAKE MY BREATH AWAY

(Love Theme)
from the Paramount Picture TOP GUN

ALTO SAX

Words and Music by GIORGIO MORODER
and TOM WHITLOCK

THAT'S AMORÉ

(That's Love)

from the Paramount Picture THE CADDY

ALTO SAX

Words by JACK BROOKS
Music by HARRY WARREN

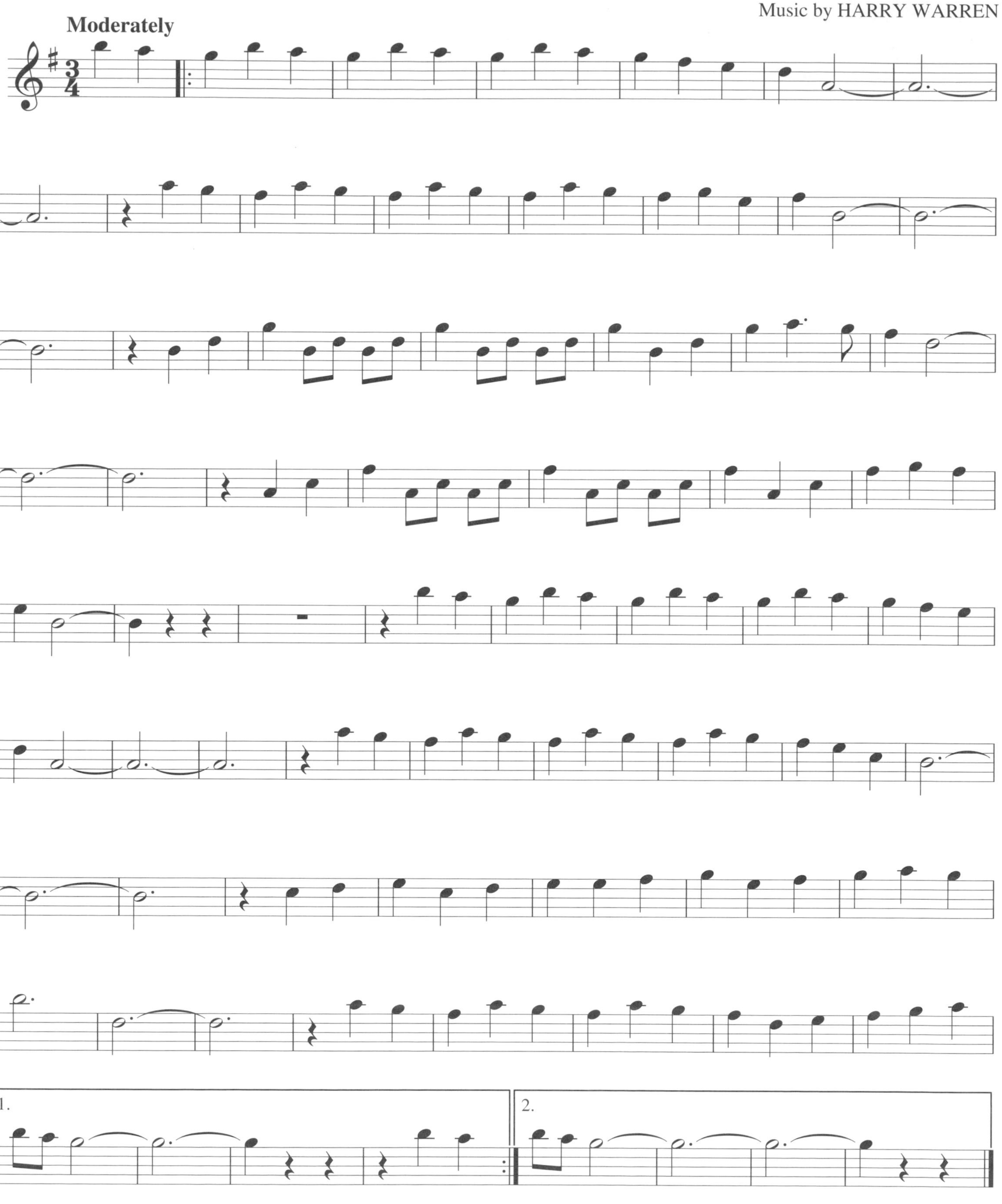

THIS LAND IS YOUR LAND

ALTO SAX

Words and Music by
WOODY GUTHRIE

Moderately bright

THOSE WERE THE DAYS

ALTO SAX

Words and Music by
GENE RASKIN

TIME AFTER TIME

ALTO SAX

Words and Music by CYNDI LAUPER
and ROB HYMAN

Moderately fast Rock

A THOUSAND MILES

ALTO SAX

Words and Music by
VANESSA CARLTON

Moderately fast

2.
D.C. al Coda
CODA

TOMORROW

from the Musical Production ANNIE

ALTO SAX

Lyric by MARTIN CHARNIN
Music by CHARLES STROUSE

TOP OF THE WORLD

ALTO SAX

Words and Music by JOHN BETTIS
and RICHARD CARPENTER

TWIST AND SHOUT

ALTO SAX

Words and Music by BERT RUSSELL
and PHIL MEDLEY

Moderately, with a beat

UNCHAINED MELODY

ALTO SAX

Lyric by HY ZARET
Music by ALEX NORTH

UNDER THE BOARDWALK

ALTO SAX

Words and Music by ARTIE RESNICK
and KENNY YOUNG

Moderately, with a beat

UNITED WE STAND

ALTO SAX

Words and Music by ANTHONY TOBY HILLER
and JOHN GOODISON

THE WAY YOU MOVE

ALTO SAX

Words and Music by ANTWAN PATTON, PATRICK BROWN and CARLTON MAHONE

Moderate groove

WE ARE THE WORLD

ALTO SAX

Words and Music by LIONEL RICHIE
and MICHAEL JACKSON

Moderately slow

WE BELONG TOGETHER

ALTO SAX

Words and Music by MARIAH CAREY,
JERMAINE DUPRI, MANUEL SEAL, JOHNTA AUSTIN,
DARNELL BRISTOL, KENNETH EDMONDS, SIDNEY JOHNSON,
PATRICK MOTEN, BOBBY WOMACK and SANDRA SULLY

To Coda
D.S. al Coda
CODA

WHAT THE WORLD NEEDS NOW IS LOVE

ALTO SAX

Lyric by HAL DAVID
Music by BURT BACHARACH

Moderate Jazz Waltz

WITH A LITTLE HELP FROM MY FRIENDS

ALTO SAX

Words and Music by JOHN LENNON
and PAUL McCARTNEY

Moderate Swing feel

WONDERFUL TONIGHT

ALTO SAX

Words and Music by
ERIC CLAPTON

WOOLY BULLY

ALTO SAX

Words and Music by
DOMINGO SAMUDIO

YELLOW SUBMARINE

ALTO SAX

Words and Music by JOHN LENNON
and PAUL McCARTNEY

YOU ARE THE SUNSHINE OF MY LIFE

ALTO SAX

Words and Music by
STEVIE WONDER

YOU RAISE ME UP

ALTO SAX

Words and Music by BRENDAN GRAHAM
and ROLF LOVLAND

YOU'VE GOT A FRIEND

ALTO SAX

Words and Music by
CAROLE KING

ZIP-A-DEE-DOO-DAH

from Walt Disney's SONG OF THE SOUTH
from Disneyland and Walt Disney World's SPLASH MOUNTAIN

ALTO SAX

Words by RAY GILBERT
Music by ALLIE WRUBEL

Brightly